Breakfast in Memphis
Vol. 3
Colors of Love

Mark Randall Mueller

Cover Art by Analy Nakat

PAPERBOOK ISBN: 979-8-9885322-5-5
EBOOK ISBN: 979-8-9885322-2-4
Library of Congress: 9798988532255
Cover Art by Analy Nakat
Instagram: @analynakat
www.analynakat.com

Breakfast in Memphis: Colors of Love

May we all experience the magic of love,
especially those who need it most.

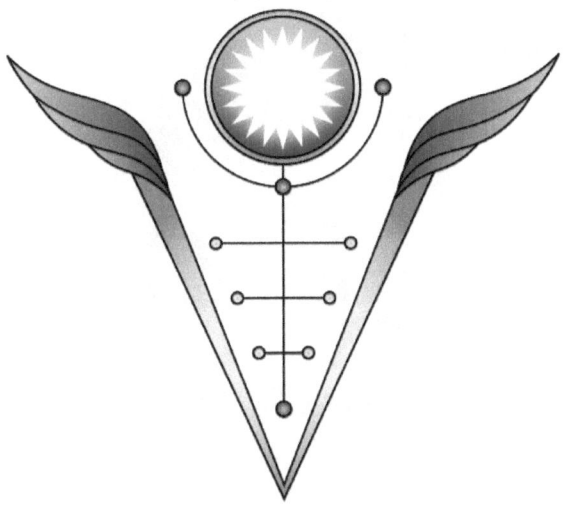

Truth and Justice League was founded from the realization that we live in an unjust and badly contaminated world and that without a positive vision for the future and the participation of ordinary people, destruction of the human species is inevitable. In the summer of 2019 we hosted a special event called the What if? Party to connect with and inspire a community of scientists, doctors, lawyers, journalists, filmmakers, environmental and social justice activists, churches, regenerative agriculturalists, artists, musicians, educators, healers, and many others to combine in their own unique ways to create a more sustainable, equitable and peaceful world.

Cont'd...

Do well by doing good. It is important to remember we are here to live free, pursue happiness and avoid hurting others through violence, carelessness, greed, toxic exposure, fraudulent business practices, discrimination, prejudice or hate.

Truth and Justice League's mission is to assist in the creative evolution of the legal system to improve the balance of fairness and justice in the lives of all people. Join us in becoming part of the solution. Let's build a better future, together we rise!

FOREWORD

Breakfast in Memphis Vol. 3: Colors of Love is a collection of poems inspired by human emotions, love, friendship, and an appreciation of the exquisite beauty and divine design of our world.

What if?
We bypassed the fear
And ignored the confusion
And do what we can do now
Without worrying about
The rest of it
Or what others have done
Or will do
And without giving any power at
All to those known or unknown
Who seek to block us, diffuse us
Defeat us or mislead us,
What if?
We started this today?
No ego, no shame, no regrets
No winners or losers
Or too small or too old
This is a co-ed team
Whatever that means in

This day and age
Gender, race, politics, religion
Educational degrees, resumes and achievements, past trauma
Past lives, personal history
Family problems, bank accounts,
Debts and credits
Leave them in the locker room
They just weigh us down
And divide us
If you need a uniform one will be provided
You pick your own number, symbol or name

Cont'd...

Who wants to play?

The field is open
I've got a ball

Keep it simple
Have fun
Like when we were kids
Imaginary is real
We have energy
And health
We are young and strong
There are no limits
Who wants in?
Say when

Aho

Wizard Bear Speaks
Breakfast in Memphis

Warning 18+

This collection of poems contains adult topics, explicit language,
raw emotional content, imaginary worlds, and harsh examination
of self and others including many political/religious/corporate and
government agencies.

(Inspired by the Ones That Will Carry On)

What I see
Tears released by love
Write words of my belief
In your greatness
And all you will achieve
I can only hope that by God's
Grace I will be there to see
It when you realize how wonderful
You are and how lucky I feel to
Have witnessed
The magic that you bring

27 Days

On the Nubian highway
Looking for a friend
Where are we going?
When will it end?
Circumstances appear
And disappear
Consequences swallow me up
And spit me out again
Lost on the road to survival
How do I find my way?
Was the magnificence
Of the past something to build upon
Or tear down and start again
27 days on the Nubian highway
Jester hats and roads of clay
One more day
In Unicorn Park
To find what I thought
Was lost
Devils and angels
Make believe
Believe and make
Alchemy of the soul
What if?
May it be so
An idea
A word
A feeling
27 days on the Nubian highway
Is the key to life
Just broken glass
Of our own past life reflections
How would we ever know?

24 Cups of Tea

24 cups of tea
On a stolen highway
Uni drew the dance card
Griffin guarded the gold
The Gypsy Queen
Directed traffic
To places no one
Understands
Sometimes magic
Happens
In the most unexpected places
And internal foreign lands
Ya mon
Night raiders heard the message
On the way to capture the queen
Ya mon
Night raiders on the way
To the castle
The queen was packed
And ready
The king was unaware
Ya mon
Rope, masks, and treasures

Cinnamon

Talked to the unicorn…
Told me she was real…
Said what's the matter darlin…
Cinnamon is my name.
Tried to get my diamonds back…
Lost 'em in the game…
Not really little ranger…
The consequence is time…
Red queen captured by a rook…
Or maybe it was a pawn…
Doesn't matter anyway…
The game is yours to win…
That's why they call me Cinnamon…
I move in any direction…
The board is just a map…
The map has many layers…
The surface is a trap…
Your wings are inspiration…
The power is your belief…
Destiny is your mission…
Don't worry about your mistakes…
Humor and grace…
Will guide you there…
And find the landing space…

Inspired by a bronze metal unicorn art car on the Playa at Burning Man

Electric Eyes

Electric eyes...and suicide...
Doesn't mean it's real...
You have to find the unicorn...
To know the final deal...
She said her name was Cinnamon...
Her wings were made of steel...

Message for the Departed

Every other Sunday
I think about you now
And when I do
I cry in gratitude
For all the love
And kindness
That we shared
In a world of
Overwhelming
Pain
A drop of blood
On a fallen leaf
My lovely soldier
Please take my grief

For Xan

It's Not My Problem

Stay in your lane
But I want to help
You're not helping
They chose it
Stay in your lane

Enter My Eyes

Brown eyes
Electric gold
Highways
Periodic tables
Just went live
How did we find
It
Without a map

(The Kelley Moment)

Love and Pain

This pain knows your name…
It travels with you…
It finds your hiding places…
You can't outwalk it…
You can't outtalk it…
You can't out drink it…
You can't throw it up…
You can't shit it out…
It taught you everything you know…
It doesn't forget…
This pain knows your friends and family…

**Intersection
(Of Unicorn Queen Avenue
And Jester King Street)**

Standing on the corner
Of your life
Waiting for the light
To change
Not what if
And could of
Been
But thank you
For the dance
And magic
And all you changed
Inside me
In time your ride
Arrives
And off you
Go into
Another dream
Through tears
I speak
Truth from joy and
Pain
Best wishes
To you truly

Louisiana Rain

Kept falling
Voodoo gods
Said more
Crows directing
Traffic
Yea
Gators keeping score
Papa Legba
Let me in
Mama
Sat me down
Your waitress will
Be right with you
Same introduction
A hundred thousand times
Before
And just like that it happened
My world now a jungle floor
A silent green dressed panther
Appeared in perfect form

Witchcraft

Witchcraft trumps
Your
Black Jack
Baby
Green panther
Blinks and
Cards fly by
Ace of rains
King of winds
Queen of lightening
Jack of thunder
City blocks go black
No more downtown power
A single streetlight in the
Sky
Hello Goddess moon

Dealer's Choice

The familiar deck of cards
Had become too comfortable
Almost routine
Life had changed
So should the game
Big cats, bright colors
Precious jewels and stones
Royal crowns on unicorns
Dancing queens all around
Jesters, jokers, magicians
Poets, artists, dancers
Musicians,
Wild cards and aces
Diamonds, emeralds,
Rubies and topaz
Jaguars and panthers
Leopards and lions
Tigers and dragons and
Always the bears
Dealer's choice
Red Queen
Are you in?

Walking Through Paradise

Walking through paradise
To get to the other side
Of town
Ya mon

Meeting of the Days

Saturday met
Tuesday
On Thursday afternoon
It was lovely
And delightful
They agreed
To meet again
As usual
Same time
Next week

Psychedelic Puddles

And a pocket full of limes
Interplanetary travel
In these most interesting
Of times
Is there an internal roadmap
To show the next exit signs
Ya mon

Junkie for Life

Is there
One more
One more hit
One more line
One more drink
One more smoke
One more fuck
One more dollar
One more dime
One more love
One more breath
Is there?
One more chance
One more
Just one
More
Day

Lullaby to a Stranger

When the day turns to darkness
And the night never ends
I'll meet you in paradise
Right down the alley
In Unicorn Park

Easter Morning 2011

It was one of those achingly beautiful mornings...
Wounded hearts sent healing currents throughout the world...
Goosebumps signaled the aliveness of spring...the presence of hope...
Musical notes floated...turned to colors...then pulsing lights and shapes...
If ever there was a time to delight in the madness and promise of life...
It is now...
The only moment we ever have...

Lessons

Trapped in your life
Is not the same as living it
Victim of circumstance
Bad parent repeating again as
Yourself or a lying lover

Tethered by Fear

Tethered by fear
And lack of imagination
We beg to survive
Another day
To somehow avoid both dying
And living
Always just seconds from drowning
In the ocean between
Me and you
Would it help
If I walked on water?

Rain in the Forest

Rain in the forest
Wet
Shimmering
Green
Trickling
Down
Branches
Dripping
From leaves
Falling
On moss
Grass
And flowers
Soaking the soil
Headed for streams
Lakes
And oceans…
What will nature do?
With man's micro-plastic
Pieces
Hitching a ride
In the human zoo

Emotional Alka-Seltzer

17 years ago
I pretended
Not to notice
You pretended
Not to care
Silent lies buried
Daily
In our efforts
To gain relief

We Walk the Edge

You lied a million times...
I lied a million one...
It all got so confusing...
I don't remember when...
Maybe it was the midnight surfing...
In the middle of the bay...
Nothing left to guide me...
Only the inner way...
Sharks, dark waves and demons...
All offered to be my friends...
What do you believe in when it really is the end?
We walk the edge...
It's what we do...

Just Around the Corner

Looking for paradise
On the south of town
Here we go again
Is it ever too late
To find
What was never lost
Again and again
Searching
Familiar
Neighborhoods
Different now
Yet frozen in time
Emotional paradise
Will you still be there
When I find you again

Colors and Shadows/Here I Am

I was red, I was blue, I was green, and I was yellow
Every color of the rainbow and
Many others in between
I would be your favorite color
I would be there with a smile
I would light your cigarette
If only you would notice
That I loved you for a while
I will not be demanding
I will treat you with respect
I would dress you up
And take you out
And fly you to Venice
For the weekend
If only you would notice
I would be your friend
In paradise
Or live with you
In Barstow
I would walk you
Through French alleys or boulevards at night
Or buy you drugs from junkies
If the price was right
I will talk with you till 3 AM
Or feed stray cats at dawn
That's who I am
I will be there for your tragedies
And glories
And forgive the unforgivable
Mistakes
Here I am
Will you see me
In the shadows or in the light of day
Here I am
Waiting for you to notice me
Here I am

(Inspired by the style of Leonard Cohen)

Breakfast in Memphis: Colors of Love

Colors of Love

Love
Is a different
Color today
Lavender turning
To gray

Silver
Meets
Purple

Just before
Dawn

Dancing on
Raindrops
Nearly
A full
Moon

Lemon Drops

Lemon drops
And sunshine
Compete in the rain
For my love's attention
At the start of the day

Love in a Blender

Love in a blender
Is difficult to separate out
Colors…flavors and
Textures all blended in
…Pain, hopes, and dreams
A thousand inventions
Thrown in between
How does it taste today?
Is it time to throw it out?
A little fruit…some ice
And a splash of madness
Who the fuck really knows
What happens next?

Flaming Arrow

Crossed the sea
Parting the waters
Stayed on course
True north
Deadly arrow
Straight for the heart

Are You With Me

Hello
Here I am
Are you with me
On this journey
Till the very end
Of time
You will be my rosebud
I will help you bloom
Nighttime calls
Believers
The days are always warm
I will meet you in the
Alley for wine
And conversation
And dancing on the edge
Of madness
In a night that never
Ends

Treasure Hunt

The treasure
Is where
We find it
Also
The pain
Deep in the mine
Or right on the surface
Elevator stopping
At
Tried to
Forget you
Moments
Preserved like fossils
In the emotional mind

Elements
Companions
Pressure
And
Time

Will You Be There?

Long time coming...
Never going to end...
Then one day...
It happens...
Your ship...
Coming in...
Rich gold treasure...
Sacred art...
Sealed orders...
Royal documents...
Maps to pleasure...music...life...
Midnight Vatican raid...
Make no mistake
Wizard Bear Captain...
Tom Ford first mate…
Emerald and black capes...
Outrageous feathers, pirate hats...
High heeled boots...
A single silver spur...
Red leather whips...
Laser pistols...
Diamond rings...
Excalibur swords...
All the best things...
Will you be here...
When the ship comes in...
Easy to run...
Think you can hide...
Can't have what you won't believe...
Midnight raids...
Stolen treasures...

Cont'd…

Can't have what you won't believe...
Wizard Bear and Tom Ford...
Sailing that ship and...
Dancing crazy...
Where will you be when the ship comes in...

Time Stands Still

Time stands still
When I am with you

Here I am
In your reflection
Standing in your golden light
Can you see my
Shadow
Smiling
As I dance between the ages
Erasing space and time
Powered by your reflection
Love's antigravity machine

Wizard Bear Speaks

Wizard Bear
Called me
Said come on down here
And listen up
I showed up to help
You a long time ago
On the road to
Burning Man
Rode shotgun on
The tour bus
I met all the girls
Walked through the desert
Stayed up all night
Danced in the moonlight
Got lost every day

I was there on the playa
When the art car
Said her name was Cinnamon
The unicorn
Please remember my name
I was there when the poems came in

Wizard Bear speaks
And so do you

Psychedelic Wine

Tripping on vibrations
Above a little alley
On the Mediterranean Sea
Sunset has so many colors
The air is bright and clear
Cats and dogs come calling
To gather with their friends
Another day in paradise
Does it ever have to end?

Reality's Edge

Dance
To the edge
Of reality
Then take it one step
Further
Into the unknown
Where no one goes
But we live
As always
Released from
The confines
Of daily existence
Can we see
What we do not know
Or remember
What we already have
Pausing for reflection
In a pool of disbelief
Shadows and light
Are not black and white

Where we go
Do we even remember
Past lives
Future selves
Is time an illusion
Doubt and fear
Complicate perfection
What we know
Is also forgotten
Sail on
In the wind
Enter the sea
Which we first came from
Unicorns and dragons
Make-believe
Sorcerer spells
Who controls
What we really believe?
Is waking up
The goal
Or the end of the dream?

ABOUT THE AUTHOR

Breakfast in Memphis Vol. 3: Colors of Love is the third in a series of poetry by Austin, Texas and Atlanta, Georgia trial lawyer, Mark Mueller. "Several years ago, these words just came into my head, unpredictably, late at night, early in the morning, while walking in downtown cities, in times of isolation, pain, loss, disappointment, crisis, love, regret, awe and joy. They often seemed to almost type themselves onto my cell phone or iPad, usually perfectly formed and complete, sometimes in pairs or bunches, and slowly they accumulated into Breakfast in Memphis."

Mark Mueller is recognized for his work in birth injury litigation and product liability cases involving damages from unsafe medical devices, chemicals and pharmaceuticals. His work has twice led to FDA safety advisories for both vacuum extractors and vaginal mesh, and then eventual removal of many dangerous transvaginal mesh devices from the market.

He successfully represented the Brave Dog Society of the Blackfoot tribe in preventing oil and gas development in a pristine national wilderness area of Montana. Mark is also counsel for the Lakota

Cont'd...

Sioux Sundance Chiefs regarding ownership rights to sacred ceremonial objects.

A number of his precedent setting, high profile cases have been featured in the national media including, most notably, Oprah, Good Morning America, Special Insider Edition, The New York Times, Texas Lawyer and National Law Journal.

Mark's production company, Voodoo Cowboy Entertainment, hosted annual musical and art performance parties for many years. Through his production company, he also served as associate/executive producer for independent films including *Downloading Nancy* (Sundance Festival), *Winter in the Blood, Slam Planet, The Two Bob's,* and Ed Brown's environmental documentary *A New Resistance.* He was a featured speaker and panelist for Conscious Media Festival programs on topics of sustainability and creating positive culture change.

Mark is currently developing a comprehensive and innovative legal strategy and support network called the Truth and Justice League. The goal of the Truth and Justice League is to address the nation's disastrous environmentally toxic legacy in ways that will hold wrongdoers accountable and lay the foundation for a more sustainable future. The hope is to restore personal freedom and democracy through active citizen involvement, jury trials, and a more informed and participatory voting public.

Mark is also the author of <u>Unicorn Park</u>, a children's poetry book, <u>Breakfast in Memphis Vol. 1: Universe Favors the Hero</u> and <u>Breakfast in Memphis Vol. 2: Midnight in the Desert</u>.

ABOUT THE ARTIST

Cover Art by Analy Nakat
Instagram: @analynakat
www.analynakat.com

Analy Nakat is a full-time artist living in Los Angeles, CA working in various mediums including painting, drawing, collaborative projects, tattoos, and music. A native of Lebanon, her family fled war and relocated to the state of Texas when she was 13, where she struggled to assimilate into American culture. At the age of 18, Analy left Texas and moved to the San Francisco Bay Area, where she studied illustration at the California College of the Arts.

Her haunting, often surreal work is revealed through a magical world that incorporates images of women, animals, plants and the patterns of nature, all of it suffused with a fascination with anthropology.

"Seeing how diverse people can live, and how people can adapt, I try to create magical places where people live in harmony with nature on canvas."

Breakfast in Memphis: Colors of Love

Find other volumes in the Breakfast in Memphis series here:

https://www.truthandjusticeleague.com/books

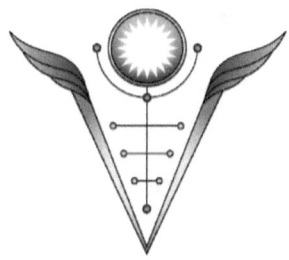